THE CHRISTIAN Life Profile™

ASSESSMENT TOOL

workbook

Praise for
The Christian Life Profile Assessment Tool

Randy Frazee is not only seriously concerned with knowing if Christians are actually growing and changing; he and his team have come up with a way to both measure and facilitate real spiritual growth. And he's depending on spiritual community to make it happen.

Larry Crabb Jr., author of *The Safest Place on Earth*

The Christian Life Profile project provides an assessment of where people are in terms of the two central dimensions of faith–love for God and love for neighbor. When these measurements are used in the context of others, in community, the findings can be enlightening, empowering, and liberating, leading to transformed lives. The Christian Life Profile assessment tool is the best tool of its kind.

George Gallup Jr., coauthor of *The Next American Spirituality*

The Christian Life Profile assessment tool and the program of discipleship focused around it is by far the best corporate plan for spiritual formation and spiritual growth that I know of in the corporate setting. It expresses the highest quality of Christian devotion, intelligence, and practical understanding of the dynamics of growth in Christ. Christian groups and leaders can be sure that resolute application of this tool in their context will progressively move their people toward realization of the goal Christ set before us: "teaching them to do all things I have commanded you." One would have to go all the way back to the "Band" groups of John Wesley to find anything that compares. Christ's plan for world revolution through the transformation of individuals and communities under his governance is still on his agenda. Adoption of this assessment tool can ensure that it is on ours as well.

Dallas Willard, author of *The Divine Conspiracy*

THE CHRISTIAN Life Profile

ASSESSMENT TOOL
workbook™

DISCOVERING THE QUALITY OF YOUR RELATIONSHIPS WITH GOD AND OTHERS IN  KEY AREAS

RANDY FRAZEE

 **ZONDERVAN**™

GRAND RAPIDS, MICHIGAN 49530 USA

ZONDERVAN™

The Christian Life Profile™ *Assessment Tool Workbook*
Copyright © 1998, 2001, 2005 by Randy Frazee

Requests for information should be addressed to:
Zondervan, *Grand Rapids, Michigan 49530*

ISBN 0-310-25161-3

Interior design by Tracey Walker

Printed in the United States of America

05 06 07 08 09 10 /❖ PAH/ 10 9 8 7 6 5 4 3 2 1

Contents

Concentrate on the four dots in the middle
of the picture for thirty-five seconds. Then
look at a white surface and keep looking
until the white circle disappears.

Foreword

George Gallup Jr.

The central challenge for Christians is embodied in Jesus Christ's "Great Commandment" from Luke 10:27: "Love the Lord your God with all your heart and with all your soul and with all your strength and with all your mind"; and "Love your neighbor as yourself."

Two key questions must be asked of Christians: *How* are you following this "Great Commandment?" and, *To what degree* are you following this "Great Commandment." If church leaders are serious about building disciples, or followers, of Jesus Christ, they need to try to gain a sense of how people are answering these questions.

Randy Frazee has responded to this vital need by offering the Christian Life Profile assessment tool as a gift to churches. With encouragement from Bob Buford of Leadership Network, as well as through consultation with local and national religious leaders, a list of thirty statements was developed, divided between a "love of God" scale and a "love of neighbor" scale. Both love dimensions were examined on the basis of beliefs (what we need to *know*), practices (what we need to *do*) and Christian virtues (what we need to *be*, described by Frazee as "the ultimate expression of Christlikeness").

This assessment tool provides a way for individuals and congregations to become "fully developing disciples." The author stresses the point that such growth can best happen in biblically based gatherings or small groups.

And what are the fruits of the application of this tool. The evidence is powerful—both for individual congregations and for society as a whole. In a nationwide Gallup Institute survey, it was discovered that those surveyed who have a deep love of God (based on the "love of God" scale) are far more likely than other Christians to say they agree with the statements "God calls me to be involved in the lives of the poor and suffering"; "I believe it is important to share the gospel faith with my neighbor because Christ has commanded me to do so"; "I pray for non-Christians to accept Jesus Christ as their Lord and Savior"; "I give away my time to serve and help others in my community", and "My first priority in spending is to support God's work."

These (and the other items on the "love of God" scale) reveal a solid connection between a deep love for God and the way people lead their lives, underscoring the transforming power of the Christian Life Profile assessment tool and pointing to the huge societal impact that could result from the widespread application of this breakthrough instrument.

George Gallup Jr., now retired, spent fifty years in the field of polling. He is a popular author of numerous books and continues to write and to lead seminars for small group ministries.

Introduction

Life Is a Journey!

Do people see a profile of Jesus Christ when they observe your life? The apostle Paul wrote in Galatians 4:19–20, "My dear children, for whom I am again in the pains of childbirth until Christ is formed in you, how I wish I could be with you now." Paul's words speak to the primary mission of the church—to see a person establish an eternal relationship with Jesus Christ that grows and develops until Christ is seen in them. The Christian Life Profile assessment tool has been created to help you in that process.

But what specifically does a follower of Christ look like? What are the characteristics or marks that form a profile of Christ in us? The Christian Life Profile assessment tool is founded on the words of Jesus in Luke 10:27, where he suggests that the essential focus of the spiritual life boils down to loving God as the first priority and loving our neighbors as ourselves. Christian maturity is primarily about relationships: with God and with others.

What are the core competencies of someone who is increasingly growing in his or her love for God and for others? This assessment tool identifies thirty core competencies. These thirty are not exhaustive but are core characteristics we see over and over again in the Bible. Of the thirty, ten are core beliefs (think like Jesus). The second set of ten competencies are core practices (act like Jesus). The final ten competencies are core virtues (be like Jesus). Our beliefs and practices are meaningless until they transform us into people whose love is seen in these ten core virtues the Bible calls "the fruit of the Spirit." We have also added "hope" and "humility" to the list found in Galatians 5. We refer to these ten core beliefs, ten core practices, and ten core virtues as the thirty core competencies.

The statements to which you will be responding seek to assess how fully you have developed this Christlike profile. Keep in mind that this tool does not compare your level of spiritual maturity with someone else's. For example, if you scored a three in prayer and another person scored a five and another a one, it doesn't mean you have grown more or less in this practice than the others. This self-assessment only compares you to the model Christ set forth. It is designed to help you discover the areas where you are the strongest, as well as the areas where you need to grow in your Christian life. The goal is for you to target a specific area you'd like to develop in your spiritual journey. As George Gallup Jr. said of this tool, "It is not so much a tool for spiritual measurement as it is a tool to create spiritual movement."

The Christian Life Profile assessment tool is most effective when used in the context of biblical community, such as a small group. The members of the group provide support, encouragement, accountability, and prayer for each other as they individually and corporately seek to grow in Christ's likeness. The assessment tool even suggests you allow three other people to answer a set of questions about you to help you in your assessment. This is one of the most beneficial aspects of this tool.

Approach this process with great anticipation and openness to the wonderful life God has in store for you as you seek to grow in the grace and knowledge of our Lord Jesus Christ.

Architecture of the Assessment Tool

Connections	Categories	Competencies
LOVE GOD	Beliefs	1. Trinity 2. Salvation by Grace 3. Authority of the Bible 4. Personal God 5. Identity in Christ 6. Church 7. Humanity 8. Compassion 9. Eternity 10. Stewardship
	Practices	1. Worship 2. Prayer 3. Bible Study 4. Single-mindedness 5. Biblical Community 6. Spiritual Gifts 7. Giving Away My Time 8. Giving Away My Money 9. Giving Away My Faith 10. Giving Away My Life
LOVE NEIGHBOR	Virtues	1. Love 2. Joy 3. Peace 4. Patience 5. Kindness/Goodness 6. Faithfulness 7. Gentleness 8. Self-control 9. Hope 10. Humility

DESCRIPTION OF THE 30 CORE COMPETENCIES

Core Competencies: beliefs

Trinity:

Creed: I believe the God of the Bible is the only true God—Father, Son, and Holy Spirit.

Key Scripture: 2 Corinthians 13:14 *"May the grace of the Lord Jesus Christ, and the love of God, and the fellowship of the Holy Spirit be with you all."*

Assessment Statements:

1. I believe the God of the Bible is the only true God. (Q. #1)
2. I believe the God of the Bible is one in essence but distinct in person—Father, Son, and Holy Spirit. (Q. #31)
3. I believe Jesus is God in the flesh—who died and rose bodily from the dead. (Q. #61)
4. I believe the Holy Spirit is God and dwells in Christians to empower them to live the Christian life. (Q. #91)

Salvation by Grace:

Creed: I believe a person comes into a right relationship with God by God's grace through faith in Jesus Christ.

Key Scripture: Ephesians 2:8–9 *"For it is by grace you have been saved, through faith—and this not from yourselves, it is the gift of God—not by works, so that no one can boast."*

Assessment Statements:

1. I believe I will inherit eternal life because of what Jesus has done for me. (Q. #2)
2. I believe nothing I do or have done can earn my salvation. (Q. #32)
3. I believe salvation comes only through Jesus Christ. (Q. #62)
4. I believe people are saved because of what Jesus Christ did, not because of what they do. (Q. #92)

Authority of the Bible:

Creed: I believe the Bible is the Word of God and has the right to command my belief and action.

Key Scripture: 2 Timothy 3:16–17 *"All Scripture is God-breathed and is useful for teaching, rebuking, correcting and training in righteousness, so that the man of God may be thoroughly equipped for every good work."*

Assessment Statements:

1. I believe the Bible is absolutely true in matters of faith and morals. (Q. #3)
2. I believe the words of the Bible are words from God. (Q. #33)
3. I believe the Bible has decisive authority over what I say and do. (Q. #63)
4. I believe the Bible is relevant to address the needs of contemporary culture. (Q. #93)

Personal God:

Creed: I believe God is involved in and cares about my daily life.

Key Scripture: Psalm 121 *"I lift up my eyes to the hills—where does my help come from? My help comes from the LORD, the Maker of heaven and earth. He will not let your foot slip—he who watches over you will not slumber; indeed, he who watches over Israel will neither slumber nor sleep. The LORD watches over you—the LORD is your shade at your right hand; the sun will not harm you by day, nor the moon by night. The LORD will keep you from all harm—he will watch over your life; the LORD will watch over your coming and going both now and forevermore."*

Assessment Statements:

1. I believe God has a purpose for my life. (Q. #4)
2. I believe pain and suffering can often bring me closer to God. (Q. #34)
3. I believe God is actively involved in my life. (Q. #64)
4. I believe God enables me to do things I could not or would not otherwise do. (Q. #94)

Identity in Christ:

Creed: I believe I am significant because of my position as a child of God.

Key Scripture: John 1:12–13 *"Yet to all who received him, to those who believed in his name, he gave the right to become children of God—children born not of natural descent, nor of human decision or a husband's will, but born of God."*

Assessment Statements:

1. I believe God loves me and therefore my life has value. (Q. #5)
2. I exist to know, love, and serve God. (Q. #35)
3. I believe God loves me, even when I do not obey him. (Q. #65)
4. I believe I am forgiven and accepted by God. (Q. #95)

Church:

Creed: I believe the church is God's primary way to accomplish his purposes on earth today.

Core Competencies: beliefs

Key Scripture: Ephesians 4:15–16 *"Instead, speaking the truth in love, we will in all things grow up into him who is the Head, that is, Christ. From him the whole body, joined and held together by every supporting ligament, grows and builds itself up in love, as each part does its work."*

Assessment Statements:

1. I believe God gives spiritual gifts to every Christian for service to the church and the community. (Q. #6)
2. I believe I cannot grow as a Christian unless I am an active member of a local church. (Q. #36)
3. I believe the community of true believers is Christ's body on earth. (Q. #66)
4. I believe the purpose of the church is to share the gospel and nurture Christians to maturity in Christ. (Q. #96)

Humanity:

Creed: I believe all people are loved by God and need Jesus Christ as their Savior.

Key Scripture: John 3:16 *"For God so loved the world that he gave his one and only Son, that whoever believes in him shall not perish but have eternal life."*

Assessment Statements:

1. I believe each person possesses a sinful nature and is in need of God's forgiveness. (Q. #7)
2. I believe we are created in the image of God and therefore have equal value, regardless of race, religion, or gender. (Q. #37)
3. I believe all people are loved by God; therefore, I too should love them. (Q. #67)
4. I believe God desires all people to have a relationship with Jesus Christ. (Q. #97)

Compassion:

Creed: I believe God calls all Christians to show compassion to those in need.

Key Scripture: Psalm 82:3–4 *"Defend the cause of the weak and fatherless; maintain the rights of the poor and oppressed. Rescue the weak and needy; deliver them from the hand of the wicked."*

Assessment Statements:

1. God calls me to be involved in the lives of the poor and suffering. (Q. #8)
2. I believe I am responsible before God to show compassion to the sick and imprisoned. (Q. #38)
3. I believe I should stand up for those who cannot stand up for themselves. (Q. #68)

4. I believe Christians should not purchase everything they can afford, so that their discretionary money can be available to help those in need. (Q. #98)

Eternity:

Creed: I believe there is a heaven and a hell, and I believe Jesus Christ is returning to judge the earth and establish his eternal kingdom.

Key Scripture: John 14:1–4 *"Do not let your hearts be troubled. Trust in God; trust also in me. In my Father's house are many rooms; if it were not so, I would have told you. I am going there to prepare a place for you. And if I go and prepare a place for you, I will come back and take you to be with me that you also may be where I am. You know the way to the place where I am going."*

Assessment Statements:

1. I believe it is important to share the gospel with my neighbor because Christ has commanded me to do so. (Q. #9)
2. I believe people who deliberately reject Jesus Christ as Savior will not inherit eternal life. (Q. #39)
3. I believe every person is subject to the judgment of God. (Q. #69)
4. I believe all people who place their trust in Jesus Christ will spend eternity in heaven. (Q. #99)

Stewardship:

Creed: I believe everything I am or own belongs to God.

Key Scripture: 1 Timothy 6:17–19 *"Command those who are rich in this present world not to be arrogant nor to put their hope in wealth, which is so uncertain, but to put their hope in God, who richly provides us with everything for our enjoyment. Command them to do good, to be rich in good deeds, and to be generous and willing to share. In this way they will lay up treasure for themselves as a firm foundation for the coming age, so that they may take hold of the life that is truly life."*

Assessment Statements:

1. I believe everything I am or own comes from God and belongs to God. (Q. #10)
2. I believe a Christian should live a sacrificial life that is not driven by pursuit of material things. (Q. #40)
3. I believe Christians should give at least 10 percent of their income to God's work. (Q. #70)
4. I believe God will bless Christians now and in the life to come for their good works. (Q. #100)

Core Competencies: practices

Worship:

Creed: I worship God for who he is and what he has done for me.

Key Scripture: Psalm 95:1–7 *"Come, let us sing for joy to the LORD; let us shout aloud to the Rock of our salvation. Let us come before him with thanksgiving and extol him with music and song. For the LORD is the great God, the great King above all gods. In his hand are the depths of the earth, and the mountain peaks belong to him. The sea is his, for he made it, and his hands formed the dry land. Come, let us bow down in worship, let us kneel before the LORD our Maker; for he is our God and we are the people of his pasture, the flock under his care."*

Assessment Statements:
1. I thank God daily for who he is and what he is doing in my life. (Q. #11)
2. I attend religious services and worship with other believers each week. (Q. #41)
3. I give God the credit for all that I am and all that I possess. (Q. #71)
4. I am not ashamed for others to know that I worship God. (Q. #101)

Prayer:

Creed: I pray to God to know him, to lay my requests before him, and to find direction for my daily life.

Key Scripture: Psalm 66:16–20 *"Come and listen, all you who fear God; let me tell you what he has done for me. I cried out to him with my mouth; his praise was on my tongue. If I had cherished sin in my heart, the Lord would not have listened; but God has surely listened and heard my voice in prayer. Praise be to God, who has not rejected my prayer or withheld his love from me!"*

Assessment Statements:
1. I seek God's will through prayer. (Q. #12)
2. I regularly confess my sins to God. (Q. #42)
3. Prayer is a central part of my daily life. (Q. #72)
4. I seek to grow closer to God by listening to him in prayer. (Q. #102)

Bible Study:

Creed: I study the Bible to know God, the truth, and to find direction for my daily life.

Key Scripture: Hebrews 4:12 *"For the word of God is living and active. Sharper than any double-edged sword, it penetrates even to dividing soul and spirit, joints and marrow; it judges the thoughts and attitudes of the heart."*

Assessment Statements:
1. I read the Bible daily. (Q. #13)
2. I regularly study the Bible to find direction for my life. (Q. #43)
3. I seek to be obedient to God by applying the truth of the Bible to my life. (Q. #73)
4. I have a good understanding of the contents of the Bible. (Q. #103)

Single-mindedness:

Creed: I focus on God and his priorities for my life.

Key Scripture: Matthew 6:33 *"But seek first his kingdom and his righteousness, and all these things will be given to you as well."*

Assessment Statements:
1. I desire Jesus Christ to be first in my life. (Q. #14)
2. I see every aspect of my life and work as service to God. (Q. #44)
3. I spend time each day reading God's Word and praying. (Q. #74)
4. I value a simple lifestyle over one cluttered with activities and material possessions. (Q. #104)

Biblical Community:

Creed: I fellowship with other Christians to accomplish God's purposes in my life, others' lives, and in the world.

Key Scripture: Acts 2:42–47 *"They devoted themselves to the apostles' teaching and to the fellowship, to the breaking of bread and to prayer. Everyone was filled with awe, and many wonders and miraculous signs were done by the apostles. All the believers were together and had everything in common. Selling their possessions and goods, they gave to anyone as he had need. Every day they continued to meet together in the temple courts. They broke bread in their homes and ate together with glad and sincere hearts, praising God and enjoying the favor of all the people. And the Lord added to their number daily those who were being saved."*

Assessment Statements:
1. I have close relationships with other Christians who have influence on my life's direction. (Q. #15)
2. I participate in a group of Christians who really know me and support me. (Q. #45)
3. I allow other Christians to hold me accountable for my actions. (Q. #75)
4. I daily pray for and support other Christians. (Q. #105)

Core Competencies: practices

Spiritual Gifts:

Creed: I know and use my spiritual gifts to fulfill God's purposes.

Key Scripture: Romans 12:4–6 *"Just as each of us has one body with many members, and these members do not all have the same function, so in Christ we who are many form one body, and each member belongs to all the others. We have different gifts, according to the grace given us."*

Assessment Statements:

1. I know my spiritual gift(s). (Q. #16)
2. I regularly use my spiritual gift(s) in ministry to accomplish God's purposes. (Q. #46)
3. I value the spiritual gifts of others to accomplish God's purposes. (Q. #76)
4. Others recognize and affirm my spiritual gift(s) and support my use of them. (Q. #106)

Giving Away My Time:

Creed: I give away my time to fulfill God's purposes.

Key Scripture: Colossians 3:17 *"And whatever you do, whether in word or deed, do it all in the name of the Lord Jesus, giving thanks to God the Father through him."*

Assessment Statements:

1. I invest my time in others by praying for them. (Q. #17)
2. I spend a good deal of time helping people with physical, emotional, or other kinds of needs. (Q. #47)
3. I give away my time to serve and help others in my community. (Q. #77)
4. I regularly volunteer at my church. (Q. #107)

Giving Away My Money:

Creed: I give away my money to fulfill God's purposes.

Key Scripture: 2 Corinthians 8:7 *"But just as you excel in everything—in faith, in speech, in knowledge, in complete earnestness and in your love for us—see that you also excel in this grace of giving."*

Assessment Statements:

1. I give away 10 percent or more of my income to God's work. (Q. #18)
2. I regularly give money to serve and help others. (Q. #48)
3. My first priority in spending is to support God's work. (Q. #78)
4. My spending habits do not keep me from giving what I feel I should give to God. (Q. #108)

Giving Away My Faith:

Creed: I give away my faith to fulfill God's purposes.

Key Scripture: Ephesians 6:19–20 *"Pray also for me, that whenever I open my mouth, words may be given me so that I will fearlessly make known the mystery of the gospel, for which I am an ambassador in chains. Pray that I may declare it fearlessly, as I should."*

Assessment Statements:

1. I frequently share my faith with people who are not Christians. (Q. #19)
2. I try to live so that others will see Christ in my life. (Q. #49)
3. I know how to share my faith with non-Christians. (Q. #79)
4. I pray for non-Christians to accept Jesus Christ as their Lord and Savior. (Q. #109)

Giving Away My Life:

Creed: I give away my life to fulfill God's purposes.

Key Scripture: Romans 12:1–2 *"Therefore, I urge you, brothers, in view of God's mercy, to offer your bodies as living sacrifices, holy and pleasing to God—this is your spiritual act of worship. Do not conform any longer to the pattern of this world, but be transformed by the renewing of your mind. Then you will be able to test and approve what God's will is—his good, pleasing and perfect will."*

Assessment Statements:

1. I am living out God's purposes for my life. (Q. #20)
2. I give up what I want to meet the needs of others. (Q. #50)
3. I give away things I possess, when I am so led by God. (Q. #80)
4. I serve God through my daily work. (Q. #110)

Core Competencies: virtues

Love:

Creed: I sacrificially and unconditionally love and forgive others.

Key Scripture: 1 John 4:10–12 *"This is love: not that we loved God, but that he loved us and sent his Son as an atoning sacrifice for our sins. Dear friends, since God so loved us, we also ought to love one another. No one has ever seen God; but if we love one another, God lives in us and his love is made complete in us."*

Assessment Statements:

1. God's grace enables me to forgive people who have hurt me. (Q. #21)
2. I rejoice when good things happen to other people. (Q. #51)
3. I demonstrate love equally toward people of all races. (Q. #81)
4. I frequently give up what I want for the sake of others. (Q. #111)

Joy:

Creed: I have inner contentment and purpose in spite of my circumstances.

Key Scripture: John 15:11 *"I have told you this so that my joy may be in you and that your joy may be complete."*

Assessment Statements:

1. I have inner contentment, even when things go wrong. (Q. #22)
2. Circumstances do not dictate my mood. (Q. #52)
3. I am excited about the sense of purpose I have for my life. (Q. #82)
4. I can be content with the money and possessions I now have. (Q. #112)

Peace:

Creed: I am free from anxiety because things are right between God, myself, and others.

Key Scripture: Philippians 4:6–7 *"Do not be anxious about anything, but in everything, by prayer and petition, with thanksgiving, present your requests to God. And the peace of God, which transcends all understanding, will guard your hearts and your minds in Christ Jesus."*

Assessment Statements:

1. I know God has forgiven me because of what Jesus has done. (Q. #23)
2. I am not angry with God, myself, or others. (Q. #53)
3. I forgive people who deeply hurt me. (Q. #83)
4. I have an inner peace from God. (Q. #113)

Patience:

Creed: I take a long time to overheat, and I endure patiently the unavoidable pressures of life.

Key Scripture: Proverbs 14:29 *"A patient man has great understanding, but a quick-tempered man displays folly."*

Assessment Statements:

1. I do not get angry with God when I have to endure suffering. (Q. #24)
2. I am known to maintain honesty and integrity when under pressure. (Q. #54)
3. I always put matters into God's hands when I am under pressure. (Q. #84)
4. I keep my composure, even when people or circumstances irritate me. (Q. #114)

Kindness/Goodness:

Creed: I choose to do the right things in my relationships with others.

Key Scripture: 1 Thessalonians 5:15 *"Make sure that nobody pays back wrong for wrong, but always try to be kind to each other and to everyone else."*

Assessment Statements:

1. I would never keep money that didn't belong to me. (Q. #25)
2. I am known as a person who speaks words of kindness to those in need of encouragement. (Q. #55)
3. I give to others, expecting nothing in return. (Q. #85)
4. I help those who are in trouble or who cannot help themselves. (Q. #115)

Core Competencies: virtues

Faithfulness:

Creed: I have established a good name with God and with others based on my long-term loyalty to that relationship.

Key Scripture: Proverbs 3:3–4 *"Let love and faithfulness never leave you; bind them around your neck, write them on the tablet of your heart. Then you will win favor and a good name in the sight of God and man."*

Assessment Statements:

1. I take unpopular stands when my faith dictates. (Q. #26)
2. I discipline my thoughts based on my faith in Jesus Christ. (Q. #56)
3. I follow God, even when it involves suffering. (Q. #86)
4. I follow through on commitments I have made to God. (Q. #116)

Gentleness:

Creed: I am thoughtful, considerate, and calm in dealing with others.

Key Scripture: Philippians 4:5 *"Let your gentleness be evident to all. The Lord is near."*

Assessment Statements:

1. I consider my own shortcomings when faced with the failures of others. (Q. #27)
2. I am known as a person who is sensitive to the needs of others. (Q. #57)
3. I am known for not raising my voice. (Q. #87)
4. I allow people to make mistakes. (Q. #117)

Self-Control:

Creed: I have power, through Christ, to control myself.

Key Scripture: Titus 2:11–13 *"For the grace of God that brings salvation has appeared to all men. It teaches us to say 'No' to ungodliness and worldly passions, and to live self-controlled, upright and godly lives in this present age, while we wait for the blessed hope—the glorious appearing of our great God and Savior, Jesus Christ."*

Assessment Statements:

1. I am not addicted to any substances—whether food, caffeine, tobacco, alcohol, or chemical. (Q. #28)
2. I do not burst out toward others in anger. (Q. #58)
3. I do not have sexual relationships that are contrary to biblical teaching. (Q. #88)
4. I control my tongue. (Q. #118)

Hope:

Creed: I can cope with the hardships of life and death because of the hope I have in Jesus Christ.

Key Scripture: Hebrews 6:19–20 *"We have this hope as an anchor for the soul, firm and secure. It enters the inner sanctuary behind the curtain, where Jesus, who went before us, has entered on our behalf."*

Assessment Statements:

1. I think a great deal about heaven and what God is preparing for me as a Christian. (Q. #29)
2. I am confident God is working everything out for my good, regardless of the circumstances today. (Q. #59)
3. My hope in God increases through my daily pursuit to live like Christ. (Q. #89)
4. My hope for the future is not found in my health or wealth, because both are so uncertain, but in God. (Q. #119)

Humility:

Creed: I choose to esteem others above myself.

Key Scripture: Philippians 2:3–4 *"Do nothing out of selfish ambition or vain conceit, but in humility consider others better than yourselves. Each of you should look not only to your own interests, but also to the interests of others."*

Assessment Statements:

1. As a child of God, I do not think too highly or too lowly of myself. (Q. #30)
2. I am not known as a person who brags. (Q. #60)
3. I am willing to make any of my faults known to Christians who care for me. (Q. #90)
4. I am not upset when my achievements are not recognized. (Q. #120)

PERSONAL ASSESSMENT

Getting Started!

Begin with Prayer

Life change is an impossible task without God working in our lives. Thankfully, for our sakes, the Bible presents life transformation as a foregone conclusion in the scope of God's desire for us. Each of us needs to realize the importance of allowing God to be the initiator of our spiritual transformation. We need to begin this assessment process by presenting ourselves as humbly dependent on him. Ask God to help you see your life clearly as you respond to each statement. Recognize that it is the Holy Spirit within the Christian who enables him or her to grow spiritually.

Assessing Your Life

The following 120 statements relate to the core beliefs, practices, and virtues of the developing disciple. Read each statement, then assess your own personal Christian experience on a scale from 0 (Does not apply at all) to 5 (Applies completely).

Here are a couple of tips that will help you better assess yourself and therefore create more effective results.

1. When you come to a statement you don't understand, mark yourself low.
2. When you come to a statement on belief, don't score yourself on whether you believe it is the right answer but rather on whether it is a way of life for you. (For example, "I believe God is actively involved in my life." You may believe this is the right answer, but you don't sense he's actually involved in your life today. If this is the case, score yourself low.)

Instructions

1. The first step is to go to the "One Another" assessments section (page 35). You'll want to pass these pages out as soon as possible so you can complete the total assessment in a timely manner. Read and follow the instructions found on page 36.
2. Detach the perforated "Scoring the Feedback" sheet on page 43.
3. Take the assessment. Write your responses to the 120 statements on the corresponding numbered space on the scoring table.
4. When you have completed the assessment, you will be guided through the measurement process to determine your results.
5. When you have completed the measurement step of the program, you will tabulate the responses of your "One Another" assessments (page 43). Reread the instructions on page 36 for assistance in completing this step.
6. You are now ready to develop a personal plan for spiritual growth (pages 46–49).

Ready to Grow? Let's Go!

Personal Assessment

	Does not apply at all		Applies somewhat		Applies completely

1. I believe the God of the Bible is the only true God.   0   1   2   3   4   5

2. I believe I will inherit eternal life because of what Jesus has done for me.   0   1   2   3   4   5

3. I believe the Bible is absolutely true in matters of faith and morals.   0   1   2   3   4   5

4. I believe God has a purpose for my life.   0   1   2   3   4   5

5. I believe God loves me and therefore my life has value.   0   1   2   3   4   5

6. I believe God gives spiritual gifts to every Christian for service to the church and the community.   0   1   2   3   4   5

7. I believe each person possesses a sinful nature and is in need of God's forgiveness.   0   1   2   3   4   5

8. God calls me to be involved in the lives of the poor and suffering.   0   1   2   3   4   5

9. I believe it is important to share the gospel with my neighbor because Christ has commanded me to do so.   0   1   2   3   4   5

10. I believe everything I am or own comes from God and belongs to God.   0   1   2   3   4   5

11. I thank God daily for who he is and what he is doing in my life.   0   1   2   3   4   5

12. I seek God's will through prayer.   0   1   2   3   4   5

13. I read the Bible daily.   0   1   2   3   4   5

14. I desire Jesus Christ to be first in my life.   0   1   2   3   4   5

15. I have close relationships with other Christians who have influence on my life's direction.   0   1   2   3   4   5

16. I know my spiritual gifts.   0   1   2   3   4   5

17. I invest my time in others by praying for them.   0   1   2   3   4   5

18. I give away 10 percent or more of my income to God's work.   0   1   2   3   4   5

19. I frequently share my faith with people who are not Christians.   0   1   2   3   4   5

Personal Assessment

	Does not apply at all		Applies somewhat		Applies completely

20. I am living out God's purposes for my life.

| 0 | 1 | 2 | 3 | 4 | 5 |

21. God's grace enables me to forgive people who have hurt me.

| 0 | 1 | 2 | 3 | 4 | 5 |

22. I have inner contentment, even when things go wrong.

| 0 | 1 | 2 | 3 | 4 | 5 |

23. I know God has forgiven me because of what Jesus has done.

| 0 | 1 | 2 | 3 | 4 | 5 |

24. I do not get angry with God when I have to endure suffering.

| 0 | 1 | 2 | 3 | 4 | 5 |

25. I would never keep money that didn't belong to me.

| 0 | 1 | 2 | 3 | 4 | 5 |

26. I take unpopular stands when my faith dictates.

| 0 | 1 | 2 | 3 | 4 | 5 |

27. I consider my own shortcomings when faced with the failures of others.

| 0 | 1 | 2 | 3 | 4 | 5 |

28. I am not addicted to any substances—whether food, caffeine, tobacco, alcohol, or chemical.

| 0 | 1 | 2 | 3 | 4 | 5 |

29. I think a great deal about heaven and what God is preparing for me as a Christian.

| 0 | 1 | 2 | 3 | 4 | 5 |

30. As a child of God, I do not think too highly or too lowly of myself.

| 0 | 1 | 2 | 3 | 4 | 5 |

31. I believe the God of the Bible is one in essence but distinct in person— Father, Son, and Holy Spirit.

| 0 | 1 | 2 | 3 | 4 | 5 |

32. I believe nothing I do or have done can earn my salvation.

| 0 | 1 | 2 | 3 | 4 | 5 |

33. I believe the words of the Bible are words from God.

| 0 | 1 | 2 | 3 | 4 | 5 |

34. I believe pain and suffering can often bring me closer to God.

| 0 | 1 | 2 | 3 | 4 | 5 |

35. I exist to know, love, and serve God.

| 0 | 1 | 2 | 3 | 4 | 5 |

36. I believe I cannot grow as a Christian unless I am an active member of a local church.

| 0 | 1 | 2 | 3 | 4 | 5 |

37. I believe we are created in the image of God and therefore have equal value, regardless of race, religion, or gender.

| 0 | 1 | 2 | 3 | 4 | 5 |

Personal Assessment

	Does not apply at all		Applies somewhat		Applies completely

38. I believe I am responsible before God to show compassion to the sick and imprisoned.   0 1 2 3 4 5

39. I believe people who deliberately reject Jesus Christ as Savior will not inherit eternal life.   0 1 2 3 4 5

40. I believe a Christian should live a sacrificial life that is not driven by pursuit of material things.   0 1 2 3 4 5

41. I attend religious services and worship with other believers each week.   0 1 2 3 4 5

42. I regularly confess my sins to God.   0 1 2 3 4 5

43. I regularly study the Bible to find direction for my life.   0 1 2 3 4 5

44. I see every aspect of my life and work as service to God.   0 1 2 3 4 5

45. I participate in a group of Christians who really know me and support me.   0 1 2 3 4 5

46. I regularly use my spiritual gift(s) in ministry to accomplish God's purposes.   0 1 2 3 4 5

47. I spend a good deal of time helping people with physical, emotional, or other kinds of needs.   0 1 2 3 4 5

48. I regularly give money to serve and help others.   0 1 2 3 4 5

49. I try to live so that others will see Christ in my life.   0 1 2 3 4 5

50. I give up what I want to meet the needs of others.   0 1 2 3 4 5

51. I rejoice when good things happen to other people.   0 1 2 3 4 5

52. Circumstances do not dictate my mood.   0 1 2 3 4 5

53. I am not angry with God, myself, or others.   0 1 2 3 4 5

54. I am known to maintain honesty and integrity when under pressure.   0 1 2 3 4 5

55. I am known as a person who speaks words of kindness to those in need of encouragement.   0 1 2 3 4 5

Personal Assessment

	Does not apply at all		Applies somewhat		Applies completely

56. I discipline my thoughts based on my faith in Jesus Christ. 0 1 2 3 4 5

57. I am known as a person who is sensitive to the needs of others. 0 1 2 3 4 5

58. I do not burst out toward others in anger. 0 1 2 3 4 5

59. I am confident God is working everything out for my good, regardless of the circumstances today. 0 1 2 3 4 5

60. I am not known as a person who brags. 0 1 2 3 4 5

61. I believe Jesus is God in the flesh—who died and rose bodily from the dead. 0 1 2 3 4 5

62. I believe salvation comes only through Jesus Christ. 0 1 2 3 4 5

63. I believe the Bible has decisive authority over what I say and do. 0 1 2 3 4 5

64. I believe God is actively involved in my life. 0 1 2 3 4 5

65. I believe God loves me, even when I do not obey him. 0 1 2 3 4 5

66. I believe the community of true believers is Christ's body on earth. 0 1 2 3 4 5

67. I believe all people are loved by God; therefore, I too should love them. 0 1 2 3 4 5

68. I believe I should stand up for those who cannot stand up for themselves. 0 1 2 3 4 5

69. I believe every person is subject to the judgment of God. 0 1 2 3 4 5

70. I believe Christians should give at least 10 percent of their income to God's work. 0 1 2 3 4 5

71. I give God credit for all that I am and all that I possess. 0 1 2 3 4 5

72. Prayer is a central part of my daily life. 0 1 2 3 4 5

73. I seek to be obedient to God by applying the truth of the Bible to my life. 0 1 2 3 4 5

Personal Assessment

	Does not apply at all		Applies somewhat		Applies completely	

74. I spend time each day reading God's Word and praying. 0 1 2 3 4 5

75. I allow other Christians to hold me accountable for my actions. 0 1 2 3 4 5

76. I value the spiritual gifts of others to accomplish God's purposes. 0 1 2 3 4 5

77. I give away my time to serve and help others in my community. 0 1 2 3 4 5

78. My first priority in spending is to support God's work. 0 1 2 3 4 5

79. I know how to share my faith with non-Christians. 0 1 2 3 4 5

80. I give away things I possess, when I am so led by God. 0 1 2 3 4 5

81. I demonstrate love equally toward people of all races. 0 1 2 3 4 5

82. I am excited about the sense of purpose I have for my life. 0 1 2 3 4 5

83. I forgive people who deeply hurt me. 0 1 2 3 4 5

84. I always put matters into God's hands when I am under pressure. 0 1 2 3 4 5

85. I give to others, expecting nothing in return. 0 1 2 3 4 5

86. I follow God, even when it involves suffering. 0 1 2 3 4 5

87. I am known for not raising my voice. 0 1 2 3 4 5

88. I do not have sexual relationships that are contrary to biblical teaching. 0 1 2 3 4 5

89. My hope in God increases through my daily pursuit to live like Christ. 0 1 2 3 4 5

90. I am willing to make any of my faults known to Christians who care for me. 0 1 2 3 4 5

91. I believe the Holy Spirit is God and dwells in Christians to empower them to live the Christian life. 0 1 2 3 4 5

Personal Assessment

	Does not apply at all		Applies somewhat		Applies completely

92. I believe people are saved because of what Jesus Christ did, not because of what they do.

    0 1 2 3 4 5

93. I believe the Bible is relevant to address the needs of contemporary culture.

    0 1 2 3 4 5

94. I believe God enables me to do things I could not or would not otherwise do.

    0 1 2 3 4 5

95. I believe I am forgiven and accepted by God.

    0 1 2 3 4 5

96. I believe the purpose of the church is to share the gospel and nurture Christians to maturity in Christ.

    0 1 2 3 4 5

97. I believe God desires all people to have a relationship with Jesus Christ.

    0 1 2 3 4 5

98. I believe Christians should not purchase everything they can afford, so that their discretionary money can be available to help those in need.

    0 1 2 3 4 5

99. I believe all people who place their trust in Jesus Christ will spend eternity in heaven.

    0 1 2 3 4 5

100. I believe God will bless Christians now and in the life to come for their good works.

    0 1 2 3 4 5

101. I am not ashamed for others to know that I worship God.

    0 1 2 3 4 5

102. I seek to grow closer to God by listening to him in prayer.

    0 1 2 3 4 5

103. I have a good understanding of the contents of the Bible.

    0 1 2 3 4 5

104. I value a simple lifestyle over one cluttered with activities and material possessions.

    0 1 2 3 4 5

105. I daily pray for and support other Christians.

    0 1 2 3 4 5

106. Others recognize and affirm my spiritual gift(s) and support my use of them.

    0 1 2 3 4 5

107. I regularly volunteer at my church.

    0 1 2 3 4 5

Personal Assessment

	Does not apply at all		Applies somewhat		Applies completely

108. My spending habits do not keep me from giving what I feel I should give to God. — 0 1 2 3 4 5

109. I pray for non-Christians to accept Jesus Christ as their Lord and Savior. — 0 1 2 3 4 5

110. I serve God through my daily work. — 0 1 2 3 4 5

111. I frequently give up what I want for the sake of others. — 0 1 2 3 4 5

112. I can be content with the money and possessions I now have. — 0 1 2 3 4 5

113. I have an inner peace from God. — 0 1 2 3 4 5

114. I keep my composure, even when people or circumstances irritate me. — 0 1 2 3 4 5

115. I help those who are in trouble or who cannot help themselves. — 0 1 2 3 4 5

116. I follow through on commitments I have made to God. — 0 1 2 3 4 5

117. I allow people to make mistakes. — 0 1 2 3 4 5

118. I control my tongue. — 0 1 2 3 4 5

119. My hope for the future is not found in my health or wealth, because both are so uncertain, but in God. — 0 1 2 3 4 5

120. I am not upset when my achievements are not recognized. — 0 1 2 3 4 5

Congratulations!

You've taken a very important first step in identifying where you are right now in your Christian life! While the material is fresh in your mind and heart, try to capture a number of the details as it relates to your experience in taking the assessment. This is simply to help you understand your thoughts, feelings, and what God may be saying to you through this personal reflection. Take just a moment and write down any memories that came to you and any areas or statements that seemed particularly sensitive or painful. Lastly, capture any thoughts or emotions you feel called to take action on now. When you finish, go to the next section, where you will begin to measure your answers.

MEASURING THE RESULTS

Measuring the Results

Instructions

Beginning at the top of the scoring table, add the rows of answers horizontally across the page (as indicated by the arrows below), writing your answer in the space to the right of the core competency associated with that row. Then, beginning at the zero (0) on the bar graph next to your total for each row, darken the line moving to the right until you reach your score for that core competency. Repeat this process for each of the thirty rows of answers.

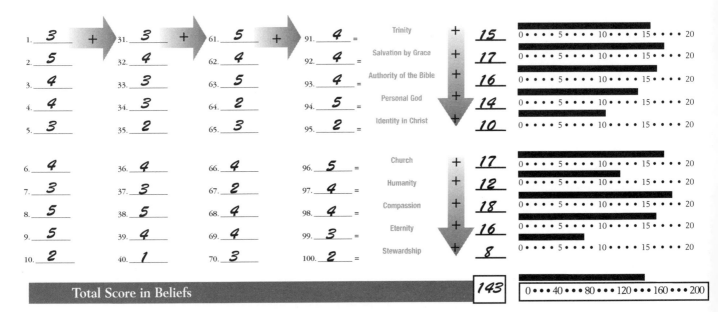

Once you've completed the horizontal scoring, begin adding the individual core competency totals vertically, placing the sum in the box beneath the last competency (143 in the example above). Do this for your scores in beliefs, practices, and virtues.

Scoring Table

1. _____	31. _____	61. _____	91. _____	=	Trinity	_____	0 • • • • 5 • • • • 10 • • • • 15 • • • • 20
2. _____	32. _____	62. _____	92. _____	=	Salvation by Grace	_____	0 • • • • 5 • • • • 10 • • • • 15 • • • • 20
3. _____	33. _____	63. _____	93. _____	=	Authority of the Bible	_____	0 • • • • 5 • • • • 10 • • • • 15 • • • • 20
4. _____	34. _____	64. _____	94 _____	=	Personal God	_____	0 • • • • 5 • • • • 10 • • • • 15 • • • • 20
5. _____	35. _____	65. _____	95. _____	=	Identity in Christ	_____	0 • • • • 5 • • • • 10 • • • • 15 • • • • 20
6. _____	36. _____	66. _____	96. _____	=	Church	_____	0 • • • • 5 • • • • 10 • • • • 15 • • • • 20
7. _____	37. _____	67. _____	97. _____	=	Humanity	_____	0 • • • • 5 • • • • 10 • • • • 15 • • • • 20
8. _____	38. _____	68. _____	98. _____	=	Compassion	_____	0 • • • • 5 • • • • 10 • • • • 15 • • • • 20
9. _____	39. _____	69. _____	99. _____	=	Eternity	_____	0 • • • • 5 • • • • 10 • • • • 15 • • • • 20
10. _____	40. _____	70. _____	100. _____	=	Stewardship	_____	0 • • • • 5 • • • • 10 • • • • 15 • • • • 20

Total Score in Beliefs   ☐   0 • • • 40 • • • 80 • • • 120 • • •160 • • •200

11. _____	41. _____	71. _____	101. _____	=	Worship	_____	0 • • • • 5 • • • • 10 • • • • 15 • • • • 20
12. _____	42. _____	72. _____	102. _____	=	Prayer	_____	0 • • • • 5 • • • • 10 • • • • 15 • • • • 20
13. _____	43. _____	73. _____	103. _____	=	Bible Study	_____	0 • • • • 5 • • • • 10 • • • • 15 • • • • 20
14. _____	44. _____	74. _____	104. _____	=	Single-mindedness	_____	0 • • • • 5 • • • • 10 • • • • 15 • • • • 20
15. _____	45. _____	75. _____	105. _____	=	Biblical Community	_____	0 • • • • 5 • • • • 10 • • • • 15 • • • • 20
16. _____	46. _____	76. _____	106. _____	=	Spiritual Gifts	_____	0 • • • • 5 • • • • 10 • • • • 15 • • • • 20
17. _____	47. _____	77. _____	107. _____	=	Giving Away My Time	_____	0 • • • • 5 • • • • 10 • • • • 15 • • • • 20
18. _____	48. _____	78. _____	108 _____	=	Giving Away My Money	_____	0 • • • • 5 • • • • 10 • • • • 15 • • • • 20
19. _____	49. _____	79. _____	109. _____	=	Giving Away My Faith	_____	0 • • • • 5 • • • • 10 • • • • 15 • • • • 20
20. _____	50. _____	80. _____	110. _____	=	Giving Away My Life	_____	0 • • • • 5 • • • • 10 • • • • 15 • • • • 20

Total Score in Practices   ☐   0 • • • 40 • • • 80 • • • 120 • • •160 • • •200

21. _____	51. _____	81. _____	111. _____	=	Love	_____	0 • • • • 5 • • • • 10 • • • • 15 • • • • 20
22. _____	52. _____	82. _____	112. _____	=	Joy	_____	0 • • • • 5 • • • • 10 • • • • 15 • • • • 20
23. _____	53. _____	83. _____	113. _____	=	Peace	_____	0 • • • • 5 • • • • 10 • • • • 15 • • • • 20
24. _____	54. _____	84. _____	114. _____	=	Patience	_____	0 • • • • 5 • • • • 10 • • • • 15 • • • • 20
25. _____	55. _____	85. _____	115. _____	=	Kindness/Goodness	_____	0 • • • • 5 • • • • 10 • • • • 15 • • • • 20
26. _____	56. _____	86. _____	116. _____	=	Faithfulness	_____	0 • • • • 5 • • • • 10 • • • • 15 • • • • 20
27. _____	57. _____	87. _____	117. _____	=	Gentleness	_____	0 • • • • 5 • • • • 10 • • • • 15 • • • • 20
28. _____	58. _____	88. _____	118. _____	=	Self-control	_____	0 • • • • 5 • • • • 10 • • • • 15 • • • • 20
29. _____	59. _____	89. _____	119. _____	=	Hope	_____	0 • • • • 5 • • • • 10 • • • • 15 • • • • 20
30. _____	60. _____	90. _____	120. _____	=	Humility	_____	0 • • • • 5 • • • • 10 • • • • 15 • • • • 20

Total Score in Virtues   ☐   0 • • • 40 • • • 80 • • • 120 • • •160 • • •200

ONE ANOTHER" ASSESSMENTS

What Is a "One Another" Assessment?

Instructions

The "One Another" assessments are a vital part of a balanced personal assessment. The "One Another" assessments are based exclusively on the Virtue core competencies. The Beliefs and Practices categories would be difficult for another person to accurately assess.

It is recommended that you carefully choose the people to whom you provide your assessments. Choose people who know you well and whose opinion you trust and respect.

The goal is to discover the truth about your Christian life. You can't grow if you don't know. You may select a variety of people to complete your assessments (i.e., a family member, a person from church or small group, a coworker, a neighbor, or a friend). Take the feedback provided as opportunities to personally grow and to become even closer to the people you've chosen to comment on your Christian walk.

Remove the perforated "One Another" assessments from the book and ask the people you've selected to complete and return the assessments by a specific date. Ask them to record their scores on the assessment, and encourage them to be as completely honest as possible.

Do not look at these assessments until after you've completed your self-assessment and tabulated the results on page 33.

When you receive the "One Another" assessments, transpose the answers from the individual assessments to the "Scoring the Feedback" sheet on page 43. Score the results in the same way as you did with your personal assessment, first adding across horizontally to determine a core competency score and then adding the totals vertically to determine a total score. Also, plot the score on the bar graphs for each of the categories.

Keep in mind that the people you choose will most likely score you higher than you do yourself. With the "One Another" feedback you're not so much looking for a total numeric score as for variations in the score. For example, if someone gave you all 5's on thirty-nine of the forty questions and only one 4, this is very significant and gives you feedback regarding an area on which you need to work.

After you finish tabulating the results of your "One Another" assessments, you are ready to develop a personal plan for spiritual growth (pages 46–49).

"One Another" Assessment

Completed by _____ for _____ Date _____

Instructions

Based on your own impressions and observations of this person's life, respond to each of the following statements. Your responses will provide valuable feedback regarding the qualities or characteristics you have or have not seen portrayed in the life of the person who asked for your assessment. On a scale from 0 (Does not apply at all) to 5 (Applies completely), how accurate are the following statements when applied to the person who asked for your assessment?

	Does not apply at all		Applies somewhat			Applies completely

1. God's grace enables him/her to forgive people who have hurt him/her.   0 1 2 3 4 5

2. He/she has an inner contentment, even when things go wrong.   0 1 2 3 4 5

3. He/she knows God has forgiven him/her because of what Jesus has done.   0 1 2 3 4 5

4. He/she does not get angry with God when he/she has to endure suffering.   0 1 2 3 4 5

5. He/she would never keep money that didn't belong to him/her.   0 1 2 3 4 5

6. He/she takes unpopular stands when his/her faith dictates.   0 1 2 3 4 5

7. He/she considers his/her own shortcomings when faced with the failures of others.   0 1 2 3 4 5

8. He/she is not addicted to any substances—whether food, caffeine, tobacco, alcohol, or chemical.   0 1 2 3 4 5

9. He/she thinks a great deal about heaven and what God is preparing for him/her as a Christian.   0 1 2 3 4 5

10. As a child of God, he/she does not think too highly or too lowly of himself/herself.   0 1 2 3 4 5

11. He/she rejoices when good things happen to other people.   0 1 2 3 4 5

12. Circumstances do not dictate his/her mood.   0 1 2 3 4 5

13. He/she is not angry with God, himself/herself, or others.   0 1 2 3 4 5

14. He/she is known to maintain honesty and integrity when under pressure.   0 1 2 3 4 5

15. He/she is known as a person who speaks words of kindness to those in need of encouragement.   0 1 2 3 4 5

16. He/she disciplines his/her thoughts based on his/her faith in Jesus Christ.   0 1 2 3 4 5

17. He/she is known as a person who is sensitive to the needs of others.   0 1 2 3 4 5

18. He/she does not burst out toward others in anger.   0 1 2 3 4 5

"One Another" Assessment

	Does not apply at all		Applies somewhat		Applies completely

19. He/she is confident God is working everything out for his/her good, regardless of the circumstances today.   0 1 2 3 4 5

20. He/she is not known as a person who brags.   0 1 2 3 4 5

21. He/she demonstrates love equally toward people of all races.   0 1 2 3 4 5

22. He/she is excited about the sense of purpose he/she has for his/her life.   0 1 2 3 4 5

23. He/she forgives people who deeply hurt him/her.   0 1 2 3 4 5

24. He/she always puts matters into God's hands when he/she is under pressure.   0 1 2 3 4 5

25. He/she gives to others, expecting nothing in return.   0 1 2 3 4 5

26. He/she follows God, even when it involves suffering.   0 1 2 3 4 5

27. He/she is known for not raising his/her voice.   0 1 2 3 4 5

28. He/she does not have sexual relationships that are contrary to biblical teaching.   0 1 2 3 4 5

29. His/her hope in God increases through his/her daily pursuit to live like Christ.   0 1 2 3 4 5

30. He/she is willing to make any of his/her faults known to Christians who care for him/her.   0 1 2 3 4 5

31. He/she frequently gives up what he/she wants for the sake of others.   0 1 2 3 4 5

32. He/she can be content with the money and possessions he/she now has.   0 1 2 3 4 5

33. He/she has an inner peace from God.   0 1 2 3 4 5

34. He/she keeps his/her composure, even when people or circumstances irritate him/her.   0 1 2 3 4 5

35. He/she helps those who are in trouble or who cannot help themselves.   0 1 2 3 4 5

36. He/she follows through on commitments he/she has made to God.   0 1 2 3 4 5

37. He/she allows people to make mistakes.   0 1 2 3 4 5

38. He/she controls his/her tongue.   0 1 2 3 4 5

39. His/her hope for the future is not found in his/her health or wealth, because both are so uncertain, but in God.   0 1 2 3 4 5

40. He/she is not upset when his/her achievements are not recognized.   0 1 2 3 4 5

"One Another" Assessment

Completed by _____ for _____ Date _____

Instructions

Based on your own impressions and observations of this person's life, respond to each of the following statements. Your responses will provide valuable feedback regarding the qualities or characteristics you have or have not seen portrayed in the life of the person who asked for your assessment. On a scale from 0 (Does not apply at all) to 5 (Applies completely), how accurate are the following statements when applied to the person who asked for your assessment?

	Does not apply at all		Applies somewhat			Applies completely

1. God's grace enables him/her to forgive people who have hurt him/her. — 0 1 2 3 4 5

2. He/she has an inner contentment, even when things go wrong. — 0 1 2 3 4 5

3. He/she knows God has forgiven him/her because of what Jesus has done. — 0 1 2 3 4 5

4. He/she does not get angry with God when he/she has to endure suffering. — 0 1 2 3 4 5

5. He/she would never keep money that didn't belong to him/her. — 0 1 2 3 4 5

6. He/she takes unpopular stands when his/her faith dictates. — 0 1 2 3 4 5

7. He/she considers his/her own shortcomings when faced with the failures of others. — 0 1 2 3 4 5

8. He/she is not addicted to any substances —whether food, caffeine, tobacco, alcohol, or chemical. — 0 1 2 3 4 5

9. He/she thinks a great deal about heaven and what God is preparing for him/her as a Christian. — 0 1 2 3 4 5

10. As a child of God, he/she does not think too highly or too lowly of himself/herself. — 0 1 2 3 4 5

11. He/she rejoices when good things happen to other people. — 0 1 2 3 4 5

12. Circumstances do not dictate his/her mood. — 0 1 2 3 4 5

13. He/she is not angry with God, himself/herself, or others. — 0 1 2 3 4 5

14. He/she is known to maintain honesty and integrity when under pressure. — 0 1 2 3 4 5

15. He/she is known as a person who speaks words of kindness to those in need of encouragement. — 0 1 2 3 4 5

16. He/she disciplines his/her thoughts based on his/her faith in Jesus Christ. — 0 1 2 3 4 5

17. He/she is known as a person who is sensitive to the needs of others. — 0 1 2 3 4 5

18. He/she does not burst out toward others in anger. — 0 1 2 3 4 5

"One Another" Assessment

	Does not apply at all		Applies somewhat		Applies completely

19. He/she is confident God is working everything out for his/her good, regardless of the circumstances today. 0 1 2 3 4 5

20. He/she is not known as a person who brags. 0 1 2 3 4 5

21. He/she demonstrates love equally toward people of all races. 0 1 2 3 4 5

22. He/she is excited about the sense of purpose he/she has for his/her life. 0 1 2 3 4 5

23. He/she forgives people who deeply hurt him/her. 0 1 2 3 4 5

24. He/she always puts matters into God's hands when he/she is under pressure. 0 1 2 3 4 5

25. He/she gives to others, expecting nothing in return. 0 1 2 3 4 5

26. He/she follows God, even when it involves suffering. 0 1 2 3 4 5

27. He/she is known for not raising his/her voice. 0 1 2 3 4 5

28. He/she does not have sexual relationships that are contrary to biblical teaching. 0 1 2 3 4 5

29. His/her hope in God increases through his/her daily pursuit to live like Christ. 0 1 2 3 4 5

30. He/she is willing to make any of his/her faults known to Christians who care for him/her. 0 1 2 3 4 5

31. He/she frequently gives up what he/she wants for the sake of others. 0 1 2 3 4 5

32. He/she can be content with the money and possessions he/she now has. 0 1 2 3 4 5

33. He/she has an inner peace from God. 0 1 2 3 4 5

34. He/she keeps his/her composure, even when people or circumstances irritate him/her. 0 1 2 3 4 5

35. He/she helps those who are in trouble or who cannot help themselves. 0 1 2 3 4 5

36. He/she follows through on commitments he/she has made to God. 0 1 2 3 4 5

37. He/she allows people to make mistakes. 0 1 2 3 4 5

38. He/she controls his/her tongue. 0 1 2 3 4 5

39. His/her hope for the future is not found in his/her health or wealth, because both are so uncertain, but in God. 0 1 2 3 4 5

40. He/she is not upset when his/her achievements are not recognized. 0 1 2 3 4 5

"One Another" Assessment

Completed by _____ for _____ Date _____

Instructions

Based on your own impressions and observations of this person's life, respond to each of the following statements. Your responses will provide valuable feedback regarding the qualities or characteristics you have or have not seen portrayed in the life of the person who asked for your assessment. On a scale from 0 (Does not apply at all) to 5 (Applies completely), how accurate are the following statements when applied to the person who asked for your assessment?

	Does not apply at all		Applies somewhat			Applies completely
1. God's grace enables him/her to forgive people who have hurt him/her.	0	1	2	3	4	5
2. He/she has an inner contentment, even when things go wrong.	0	1	2	3	4	5
3. He/she knows God has forgiven him/her because of what Jesus has done.	0	1	2	3	4	5
4. He/she does not get angry with God when he/she has to endure suffering.	0	1	2	3	4	5
5. He/she would never keep money that didn't belong to him/her.	0	1	2	3	4	5
6. He/she takes unpopular stands when his/her faith dictates.	0	1	2	3	4	5
7. He/she considers his/her own shortcomings when faced with the failures of others.	0	1	2	3	4	5
8. He/she is not addicted to any substances—whether food, caffeine, tobacco, alcohol, or chemical.	0	1	2	3	4	5
9. He/she thinks a great deal about heaven and what God is preparing for him/her as a Christian.	0	1	2	3	4	5
10. As a child of God, he/she does not think too highly or too lowly of himself/herself.	0	1	2	3	4	5
11. He/she rejoices when good things happen to other people.	0	1	2	3	4	5
12. Circumstances do not dictate his/her mood.	0	1	2	3	4	5
13. He/she is not angry with God, himself/herself, or others.	0	1	2	3	4	5
14. He/she is known to maintain honesty and integrity when under pressure.	0	1	2	3	4	5
15. He/she is known as a person who speaks words of kindness to those in need of encouragement.	0	1	2	3	4	5
16. He/she disciplines his/her thoughts based on his/her faith in Jesus Christ.	0	1	2	3	4	5
17. He/she is known as a person who is sensitive to the needs of others.	0	1	2	3	4	5
18. He/she does not burst out toward others in anger.	0	1	2	3	4	5

"One Another" Assessment

	Does not apply at all		Applies somewhat		Applies completely

19. He/she is confident God is working everything out for his/her good, regardless of the circumstances today.   0 1 2 3 4 5

20. He/she is not known as a person who brags.   0 1 2 3 4 5

21. He/she demonstrates love equally toward people of all races.   0 1 2 3 4 5

22. He/she is excited about the sense of purpose he/she has for his/her life.   0 1 2 3 4 5

23. He/she forgives people who deeply hurt him/her.   0 1 2 3 4 5

24. He/she always puts matters into God's hands when he/she is under pressure.   0 1 2 3 4 5

25. He/she gives to others, expecting nothing in return.   0 1 2 3 4 5

26. He/she follows God, even when it involves suffering.   0 1 2 3 4 5

27. He/she is known for not raising his/her voice.   0 1 2 3 4 5

28. He/she does not have sexual relationships that are contrary to biblical teaching.   0 1 2 3 4 5

29. His/her hope in God increases through his/her daily pursuit to live like Christ.   0 1 2 3 4 5

30. He/she is willing to make any of his/her faults known to Christians who care for him/her.   0 1 2 3 4 5

31. He/she frequently gives up what he/she wants for the sake of others.   0 1 2 3 4 5

32. He/she can be content with the money and possessions he/she now has.   0 1 2 3 4 5

33. He/she has an inner peace from God.   0 1 2 3 4 5

34. He/she keeps his/her composure, even when people or circumstances irritate him/her.   0 1 2 3 4 5

35. He/she helps those who are in trouble or who cannot help themselves.   0 1 2 3 4 5

36. He/she follows through on commitments he/she has made to God.   0 1 2 3 4 5

37. He/she allows people to make mistakes.   0 1 2 3 4 5

38. He/she controls his/her tongue.   0 1 2 3 4 5

39. His/her hope for the future is not found in his/her health or wealth, because both are so uncertain, but in God.   0 1 2 3 4 5

40. He/she is not upset when his/her achievements are not recognized.   0 1 2 3 4 5

Scoring the Feedback

1. _____	11. _____	21. _____	31. _____	=	Love	_____	0 • • • 5 • • • 10 • • • 15 • • • 20
2. _____	12. _____	22. _____	32. _____	=	Joy		0 • • • 5 • • • 10 • • • 15 • • • 20
3. _____	13. _____	23. _____	33. _____	=	Peace		0 • • • 5 • • • 10 • • • 15 • • • 20
4. _____	14. _____	24. _____	34. _____	=	Patience		0 • • • 5 • • • 10 • • • 15 • • • 20
5. _____	15. _____	25. _____	35. _____	=	Kindness/Goodness		0 • • • 5 • • • 10 • • • 15 • • • 20
6. _____	16. _____	26. _____	36. _____	=	Faithfulness		0 • • • 5 • • • 10 • • • 15 • • • 20
7. _____	17. _____	27. _____	37. _____	=	Gentleness		0 • • • 5 • • • 10 • • • 15 • • • 20
8. _____	18. _____	28. _____	38. _____	=	Self-control		0 • • • 5 • • • 10 • • • 15 • • • 20
9. _____	19. _____	29. _____	39. _____	=	Hope		0 • • • 5 • • • 10 • • • 15 • • • 20
10. _____	20. _____	30. _____	40. _____	=	Humility		0 • • • 5 • • • 10 • • • 15 • • • 20

Total Score in Virtues

[ ]   0 • • • 40 • • • 80 • • • 120 • • • 160 • • • 200

1. _____	11. _____	21. _____	31. _____	=	Love	_____	0 • • • 5 • • • 10 • • • 15 • • • 20
2. _____	12. _____	22. _____	32. _____	=	Joy		0 • • • 5 • • • 10 • • • 15 • • • 20
3. _____	13. _____	23. _____	33. _____	=	Peace		0 • • • 5 • • • 10 • • • 15 • • • 20
4. _____	14. _____	24. _____	34. _____	=	Patience		0 • • • 5 • • • 10 • • • 15 • • • 20
5. _____	15. _____	25. _____	35. _____	=	Kindness/Goodness		0 • • • 5 • • • 10 • • • 15 • • • 20
6. _____	16. _____	26. _____	36. _____	=	Faithfulness		0 • • • 5 • • • 10 • • • 15 • • • 20
7. _____	17. _____	27. _____	37. _____	=	Gentleness		0 • • • 5 • • • 10 • • • 15 • • • 20
8. _____	18. _____	28. _____	38. _____	=	Self-control		0 • • • 5 • • • 10 • • • 15 • • • 20
9. _____	19. _____	29. _____	39. _____	=	Hope		0 • • • 5 • • • 10 • • • 15 • • • 20
10. _____	20. _____	30. _____	40. _____	=	Humility		0 • • • 5 • • • 10 • • • 15 • • • 20

Total Score in Virtues

[ ]   0 • • • 40 • • • 80 • • • 120 • • • 160 • • • 200

1. _____	11. _____	21. _____	31. _____	=	Love	_____	0 • • • 5 • • • 10 • • • 15 • • • 20
2. _____	12. _____	22. _____	32. _____	=	Joy		0 • • • 5 • • • 10 • • • 15 • • • 20
3. _____	13. _____	23. _____	33. _____	=	Peace		0 • • • 5 • • • 10 • • • 15 • • • 20
4. _____	14. _____	24. _____	34. _____	=	Patience		0 • • • 5 • • • 10 • • • 15 • • • 20
5. _____	15. _____	25. _____	35. _____	=	Kindness/Goodness		0 • • • 5 • • • 10 • • • 15 • • • 20
6. _____	16. _____	26. _____	36. _____	=	Faithfulness		0 • • • 5 • • • 10 • • • 15 • • • 20
7. _____	17. _____	27. _____	37. _____	=	Gentleness		0 • • • 5 • • • 10 • • • 15 • • • 20
8. _____	18. _____	28. _____	38. _____	=	Self-control		0 • • • 5 • • • 10 • • • 15 • • • 20
9. _____	19. _____	29. _____	39. _____	=	Hope		0 • • • 5 • • • 10 • • • 15 • • • 20
10. _____	20. _____	30. _____	40. _____	=	Humility		0 • • • 5 • • • 10 • • • 15 • • • 20

Total Score in Virtues

[ ]   0 • • • 40 • • • 80 • • • 120 • • • 160 • • • 200

PERSONAL PLAN FOR
SPIRITUAL GROWTH

Personal Plan for Spiritual Growth

Instructions

Now that you've completed your personal assessment and solicited the feedback of three other people, you are ready to develop a targeted plan for spiritual growth.

Remember, God desires to work a healthy balance into our lives; so we want to discover the areas in our Christian experience where we are deficient. So many Christians continue to build only on their strengths and never address areas of weakness. The objective is to discover where in your life God wants to initiate change and then develop a goal for personal growth, along with a specific, measurable plan to realize this goal.

Celebrating Your Strengths

1. Looking at your personal assessment score (page 33), what is your strongest competency in each area? After each one, summarize your thoughts on why this is an area of strength for you.

    Beliefs: _____

    Practices:_____

    Virtues: _____

2. Looking at the scores for your "One Another" assessments (page 43), add together the three scores for each virtue. In what three areas were you scored the highest? After each one, summarize your thoughts on why this is an area of strength for you.

    Virtue: _____

    Virtue: _____

    Virtue: _____

3. Compare your personal assessment of your strengths with the "One Another's." Are they the same? Are they different? Record your thoughts below.

    _____

    _____

    _____

    _____

    _____

    _____

    _____

Targeting Your Growth Area

1. Looking at your personal assessment score (page 33), what are your lowest scores in each area? After each one, summarize your thoughts on why this is an area of weakness for you. Look at your scores for each individual statement. Is there a belief, practice, or virtue on which you scored particularly low on one statement as compared to the other three? If so, look back at that assessment statement and write it in the space provided below. This will aid you in targeting a more specific area for growth.

    Beliefs: _____

    _____

    Practices: _____

    _____

Personal Plan for Spiritual Growth

Virtues: _____

_____

2. Do you see any relationship or connection between these three areas?

_____

_____

_____

3. Looking at the scores for your "One Another" assessments (page 43), in what three areas did your assessors score you the lowest? A good idea is to probe with them in person why they gave you low ratings in this area. Make sure you give them the freedom to share frankly with you. After each of the three areas, summarize their thoughts on why this is an area of weakness for you. If there is one statement for which they scored you particularly low as compared to the other three statements in a given area, write that statement in the space provided below. This will aid you in targeting a more specific area for growth.

Virtue: _____

_____

_____

Virtue: _____

_____

_____

Virtue: _____

_____

_____

4. Compare the lowest area on your personal assessment with the "One Another's." Are they the same? Are they different? Record your thoughts below.

_____

_____

_____

_____

5. In the space below, identify just one core competency you desire to concentrate on over the next year. If it is one specific statement from the assessment, write that down as well. It can be a belief, a practice, or a virtue. Before you make your final selection, spend time in meditation and prayer. Explain why you chose this competency.

_____

_____

_____

_____

_____

_____

_____

Personal Plan for Spiritual Growth

My Personal Plan for Spiritual Growth

Today's Date:_____

Over the next twelve months, I, _____,
(insert your name)

with the help of my God and community, intend to grow in the area of:

_____
(category, competency, specific statement, or creed)

by (record the specific action steps you have selected from the recommended resources on page 52):

1. _____

2. _____

3. _____

4. _____

5. _____

The three people I am asking to encourage me, pray for me, and hold me accountable to accomplish this goal are:

Name:_____ Signature of Person: _____

Name:_____ Signature of Person: _____

Name:_____ Signature of Person: _____

How did I do? (One year from now sit down with the three people above and evaluate your progress. Record your combined thoughts below).

_____

_____

_____

_____

_____

_____

_____

_____

_____

Personal Plan for Spiritual Growth

My Personal Plan for Growth

1. Refer to "My Personal Plan for Spiritual Growth" on page 48. Take a moment now to reflect on the area you've targeted. First, write out the category (beliefs, practices, virtues). Second, identify the core competency (for example, Trinity, Prayer, Peace). Finally, if applicable, write out the specific statement you are targeting (for example, "I allow people to make mistakes" [Q. #117]). If there is not one specific question, simply write down the Creed for that area found on pages 14 to 19 (for example, "I am thoughtful, considerate, and calm in dealing with others" [Creed for Gentleness]).

2. Now carefully read page 52. This will help you understand the relationship between the beliefs, practices, and virtues. For example, while you may have identified a virtue as your targeted area, you may choose a resource in a beliefs area or practices area because growth in that area can be essential to maximize your growth in the virtue selected.

3. Go to the website www.theconnectingchurch.com and look at the recommended resources and ideas for the specific area you selected, as well as the resources and ideas from the related categories from your discovery above. Select at least one and no more than five specific action steps you intend to take over the next twelve months to grow in your targeted area.

4. Identify three people to help you through prayer, encouragement, and gentle accountability. Ask them to sign their name on the appropriate line. Make a copy of your personal plan for each of them to keep.

5. Share your discoveries and your personal plan for spiritual growth with the members of your small group.

6. Keep your personal plan in a place where you can review it regularly (in your Bible, in your planner, posted on a bulletin board). Lay this plan before you as you pray, asking God to give you insight, discipline, and strength.

7. In one year evaluate your progress. Record your thoughts in the space provided on page 46 about how you think you did over the course of the year. Don't forget to include feedback from the three people you asked to help you accomplish this goal.

RESOURCES FOR
TARGETED GROWTH

Resources for Targeted Growth

This section of the Christian Life Profile assessment tool guides you in selecting specific action steps that will help you grow in your targeted area. In a moment you will be looking at some recommended ideas, suggestions, and resources for the competency you desire to develop. Your objective here is to select from one to five action steps to cultivate growth. You will record them in your personal plan for spiritual growth on page 46.

Before you do so, you'll want to probe the connection between the beliefs, practices, and virtues. Most people will score themselves the highest in beliefs and the lowest in practices and virtues. How about you? Look back over your score to see if this was true for you.

Our belief system is foundational to the development of our Christian practices and virtues. Consider the following illustration:

	are developed through	which produce
Beliefs...Practices................................Virtues		

For example, if we struggle in the area of *humility*, we may want to look at our *identity in Christ* score. When our identity is based on our performance and not in our position in Christ, we feel a need to brag and tout our accomplishments or to dominate a conversation. One of the greatest ways to enhance Christlike humility in our lives is to improve our knowledge and belief in our identity in Christ. There are a number of possible connections. Our struggle with *worship* may have to do with an inadequate view of God (the *Trinity*). Our struggle with love might involve not seeing other people as God sees them (*humanity*).

Take some time to probe the gap between your beliefs, practices, and virtues. If you scored high in the beliefs but low in the practices or virtues, look at your scores in the related areas. It is likely that some of your action steps for the next twelve months will come from other areas. For example, if your selected area for targeted growth is *worship*, you may seek to grow in your belief in the *Trinity* (your understanding of God). The list below is only a partial listing of connections. Feel free to probe other connections. (By the way, it may really help to dialogue out loud with others about this.)

beliefs	practices	virtues
Trinity	worship	humility, peace, hope
salvation by grace	giving away my faith	peace
authority of the Bible	Bible study	self-control
personal God	prayer	joy
identity in Christ	worship, prayer	humility
church	biblical community, spiritual gifts	faithfulness
humanity	giving away my faith	love, gentleness
compassion	giving away my time	kindness/goodness
eternity	giving away my faith	hope
stewardship	giving away my money/life, single-mindedness	humility, faithfulness, self-control

For a listing of up-to-date resources for each of the thirty core competencies, go to www.theconnectingchurch.com.

A GUIDE FOR SMALL
GROUP DISCUSSION

A Guide for Small Group Discussion

The Christian Life Profile assessment tool is optimized when it is shared with a small group of fellow Christians. If you are the leader of a small group, you can use the outline below to assist your group in sharing the results of their assessment with each other.

Preparing

1. James 5:16 tells us, "Confess your sins to each other and pray for each other so that you may be healed. The prayer of a righteous man is powerful and effective." This biblical practice is a missing component in most contemporary Christian communities. The Christian Life Profile assessment tool seeks to assist in the healthy restoration of this function.

2. Most people in your group should feel comfortable sharing the results of their profile with the whole group. However, you may have some who are too intimidated, are new to the group, or have had a bad experience in the past with vulnerability. As the leader you need to find out which group members will share the results with the entire group. Those who don't feel comfortable should not be pressured. Consider seeing if they are willing to share the results one-on-one with you, as the leader, or with someone else in the group. Later, when the person is ready, he or she can share with the whole group. Please stress to all group members that everything shared is strictly confidential.

3. Assign a date for people to share their profiles with the group. Essentially, they will be sharing their answers from the "Personal Plan for Spiritual Growth" section (pages 46–49). It takes a minimum of thirty minutes and a maximum of sixty minutes to share one profile.

Sharing

1. The person assigned begins by sharing his or her strengths as recorded in the "Personal Plan for Spiritual Growth" section ("Celebrating Your Strengths," page 46).

2. Members of the group should take time to celebrate that person by sharing their positive experiences with him or her. This should be a totally uplifting time for that person. For example, another group member may say, "John, I affirm that you are strong in prayer. I remember a time when ... "

3. The person then shares his or her areas of greatest struggle ("Targeting Your Growth Area," pages 46–47). It is very important that other group members not dismiss a person's confession. Other members should not say things like, "Oh, I really don't see that in you." Group members should interact and ask questions in a sensitive manner.

4. The person now shares the area in which he or she is trusting God for growth over the next twelve months ("My Personal Plan for Spiritual Growth," page 48). Reinforce the need to have a specific and measurable plan for growing in this area. Also, find out which three people he or she has asked or plans to ask to sign this plan to help him or her reach this goal.

A Guide for Small Group Discussion

Praying

1. When the person is done sharing, gather around that person to pray over him or her.

2. In the prayer, celebrate that person's life, strengths, desire to grow in the selected areas, and the group's commitment to support him or her in this journey.

Probing Deeper

1. If your group desires, you can use the following suggestions to probe the results of the profile more deeply.

2. Probe your assessment for cause-effect relationships. Take an area you scored low in, and look at other beliefs, practices, and virtues that are also low to see what role they may play in influencing your development in this area.

3. Probe the gap between beliefs, practices, and virtues. If you scored high in the beliefs but low in the practices or virtues, then you may want to probe the actual depth of your beliefs. There is a difference between really believing something and simply thinking it is the right answer for Christians to give. Consider the possible connections below between the beliefs, practices, and virtues.

beliefs	practices	virtues
Trinity	worship	humility, peace, hope
salvation by grace	giving away my faith	peace
authority of the Bible	Bible study	self-control
personal God	prayer	joy
identity in Christ	worship, prayer	humility
church	biblical community, spiritual gifts	faithfulness
humanity	giving away my faith	love, gentleness
compassion	giving away my time	kindness/goodness
eternity	giving away my faith	hope
stewardship	giving away my money/life, single-mindedness	humility, faithfulness, self-control

4. Probe the "One Another's." Take the time to look at your "One Another" assessments globally.

    a. Probe the areas where the "One Another's" differ.

        For example, if only one person scored you low on the statement "He/she allows people to make mistakes," maybe you only fail to do this in your relationship with that person. You may want to talk further with him or her about this.

    b. Probe what it may mean if someone gave you all 4's and 5's. It could mean you mentored or discipled him or her and he or she idolizes you. Perhaps it would be wise to have someone else do your assessment as well. It could also mean they don't feel safe telling you the truth. It could simply mean they don't like to be confrontational in any way. Pray about talking to him or her regarding this issue. Keep in mind that most people will rate you higher than you rated yourself. Don't look at the numbers but at the dips in the numbers.

        For example, if they gave you a 5 on most things and then gave you a 4 or 3 in an area, they are likely sending you a big message, even though you may have scored yourself lower.

Following Up

1. Each group member should write down the other members' growth plans on a sheet of paper. You can use the "Prayer Guide for Group Members" on the next page if you like. Be sure to use it respectfully and confidentially. You may encourage everyone to use initials instead of actual names for their list.

2. About once a month, you can ask that person to give an update on how things are going. It's usually a good idea to let them know ahead of time that it will be their turn to share, so they'll be ready to give a good update. Use this as an opportunity to encourage, pray over, or even gently challenge each other.

3. Commit as a group to taking the profile exactly one year from the time you first took it. Compare the results next year with what happened this year. The findings should be most helpful and encouraging.

Prayer Guide for Group Members

Below is the list of the names (or initials) of the people who took the Christian Life Profile assessment tool with me. There is space provided for writing down the area they are targeting for growth over the next year. I commit to supporting and praying for them as they take this awesome journey to think, act, and become more like Jesus Christ.

NAME	AREA OF TARGETED GROWTH	COMMENTS
1.		
2.		
3.		
4.		
5.		
6.		
7.		
8.		
9.		
10.		

The Story behind the Christian Life Profile Assessment Tool

The tool you hold in your hand has taken ten years to develop. It is a labor of love and a passion for Christ of many people.

The Initial Challenge: Bob Buford, founder of Leadership Network and author of *Halftime*, gave the initial challenge to pastors to "measure the mission." If our mission is to produce followers of Christ, said Buford, then we need some indication that it's actually happening in people's lives. I was captivated by this vision and took Buford up on his challenge. As Bob has done with so many projects, he put his money where his mouth is and funded the work. Plain and simple, this tool would not be in your hands today without Bob's obedience to Christ and his passion to produce "fruit that grows on others' trees."

The Initial Team: Three teams came together to tackle the assignment—Pantego Bible Church of Forth Worth, Texas; Willow Creek Community Church of South Barrington, Illinois; and the South Carolina Southern Baptist Convention. While each of us worked to develop our own model, we freely shared invaluable ideas and insights with each other.

The Source behind the Thirty Core Competencies: The Bible is the sole source behind the selection of the thirty core competencies. Dozens of people scrolled through the Bible over and over again to find the core, repeatable characteristics of a follower of Christ. The structure of beliefs, practices, and virtues was birthed out of *The Saints Among Us* by George Gallup Jr. and Timothy Jones. The initial idea of building the thirty core competencies around the greatest commandment—love God and love our neighbor—came from Winton Manning, former senior vice president of Educational Testing Service in Princeton, New Jersey.

The Development of the Tool: The first edition of this tool was created out of multiple brainstorming meetings I had with George Gallup Jr. in Dallas, Texas, and Princeton, New Jersey. Several people joined us at these gatherings, including Bob Buford, Scott Jones, Alan Klaas, Gerald McDermott, Larry Nelson, and John Williams, to name a few. I have fond memories of the long days in the Gun Room of the Nassau Club with these folks.

Testing and Refining: Several people over the years have graciously offered their input and assistance in making this a first-class tool. Dallas Willard, J. I. Packer, and Larry Crabb gave insightful feedback on the theology and the recommended communal approach. George Barna gave us feedback on the structure of the tool, which took the quality to another level. Alan Klaas tested the tool in twenty churches to ensure that the questions were effective in helping people identify their spiritual strengths and gaps in their journeys to become followers of Christ. Gerald McDermott gathered an ecumenical group of leaders from the Catholic Church and all the major Protestant denominations to ensure that the language was as inclusive as possible. For example, the tool was originally called "The Spiritual Growth Indicator." These leaders gave compelling reasons to call it "The Christian Life Profile Assessment Tool."

This tool has been through five revisions and editions. Many people helped along the way—John Castle, Gary Lawrence, Rozanne Frazee, Vince Leone, Greg Pettigrew, Rita Ballow, Ruth Bulick, Maria Garman, and the wonderful staff members of Pantego Bible Church, to name a few. The congregation of Pantego Bible Church, where I serve as senior pastor, has graciously tested each edition of this tool with great patience. Over the last ten years, hundreds of churches and organizations have used this tool and have provided great insights on how to improve it.

The Story behind the Christian Life Profile Assessment Tool

The Spiritual State of the Union: The University of Pennsylvania asked The Gallup Organization to help them measure and provide an ongoing benchmark of the "spiritual temperature" in America. One of the indicators chosen was the thirty core competencies. For more information on the results and findings, contact The Gallup Organization in Princeton, New Jersey.

The Finished Product: Through my partnership with Zondervan, we have been able to provide a full training kit for those who desire to use this tool in their church, small group, university, or organization. My desire is that you will be able to use this assessment to accomplish the Galatians 4:19 vision in your own life and in the lives of the people you serve: "until Christ is formed in you."

Randy Frazee, Fort Worth, Texas

The Connecting Church
Beyond Small Groups to Authentic Community

Forewords by Larry Crabb, George Gallup Jr., and Dallas Willard

Randy Frazee

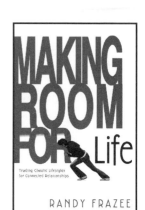

The development of meaningful relationships, where every member carries a significant sense of belonging, is central to what it means to be the church. So why do many Christians feel disappointed and disillusioned with their efforts to experience authentic community? Despite the best efforts of pastors, small group leaders, and faithful laypersons, church too often is a place of loneliness rather than connection.

Church can be so much better. So intimate and alive. *The Connecting Church* tells you how. The answer may seem radical today, but it was a central component of life in the early church. First-century Christians knew what it meant to live in vital community with one another, relating with a depth and commitment that made "the body of Christ" a perfect metaphor for the church. What would it take to reclaim that kind of love, joy, support, and dynamic spiritual growth? Read this book and find out.

Hardcover: 0-310-23308-9

Making Room for Life
Trading Chaotic Lifestyles for Connected Relationships

Randy Frazee

What if you could . . .
- Get all your work done by 6:00 p.m.?
- Eat dinner with your family every night?
- Form deep, satisfying relationships?
- Naturally blend the world of church with your everyday life?
- Spend hours a week on your hobbies?

You can! *Making Room for Life* reveals how to make all of these things a reality. Not by working faster or having more gadgets, but by simply choosing a lifestyle of conversation and community over a lifestyle of accumulation.

Randy Frazee's practical, motivating insights call you back to the kind of relationships and life rhythms you were created to enjoy. In *Making Room for Life*, Frazee shows you how—and why it's so important—to balance work and play, establish healthy boundaries, deal with children's activities and homework, bring Jesus to your neighbors, and build authentic bonds with a circle of close friends.

Share these insights with those around you and help usher in an amazing transformation: your life and the lives of others blooming—in the midst of the chaos and fragmentation of today's culture—into communities of purpose and peace.

Hardcover: 0-310-25016-1

Unabridged Audio Pages® Cassette: 0-310-25685-2

Unabridged Audio Pages® CD: 0-310-25686-0

Pick up a copy today at your favorite bookstore!

ZONDERVAN™

GRAND RAPIDS, MICHIGAN 49530 USA

WWW.ZONDERVAN.COM

We want to hear from you. Please send your comments about this book to us in care of zreview@zondervan.com. Thank you.

GRAND RAPIDS, MICHIGAN 49530 USA

WWW.ZONDERVAN.COM